Anxiety

A Step By Step Guide To Achieving Inner Calm:
Overcoming Mood Disorders And Anxiety Through
Mindfulness And Acceptance

*(How To Stop Being Restless, Stop Thinking Too Much
After Betrayal, And Useful Anxiety Relieving Techniques)*

AntoninoMonreal

TABLE OF CONTENT

Introduction 1

Being Aware Of The Things That Set Off Your Reactions 6

How Does Society Play A Role In The Development Of Women's Social Anxiety? 11

The Importance Of Technology And Social Media In The Role 19

Which School Of Thought Within Psychology Best Describes Emotional Intelligence? 38

The Importance Of Self-Care In The Maintenance Of Mental Health 57

Creating And Nurturing Beneficial Relationships 66

Variations In Hormone Levels 69

Benefits Of Positive Affirmations For Those Struggling With Sleep Anxiety 75

Aspects Of The Natural World 80

Illustrations From Everyday Life 84

Foods That Are Good For Your Mental Health 92

Additional Methods Of Caring For Oneself 100

Methods That Can Help Improve One's Social Abilities.......................... 104

The Path To Serenity: Recognizing The Importance Of Mindfulness 107

Anxiety Disorders Can Take Many Forms. 113

Challenges To Communication In Relationships Caused By Attention Deficit Hyperactivity Disorder...................... 122

The Acronym "Cbt" Stands For Cognitive Behavioral Therapy................................. 125

Incorporating Mindfulness: Some Useful Pointers And Advice................................ 133

Practices That Can Help Clear Your Mind And Reduce The Mental Clutter You Experience On A Day-To-Day Basis Include: 136

Increasing One's Own Self-Esteem 141

Share What You Have To Offer With The World. 155

Things That People Who Suffer From Social Anxiety Want To Have........................... 159

Physical Experiences While Surfing................. 167

Introduction

There is a good chance that you are already familiar with the cortex, which is the portion of the brain that occupies the top part of the skull. It is the part of the brain that is responsible for thinking, and some people believe that it is the part of the brain that is responsible for making us human. This is because it enables us to reason, form language, and take part in complicated speculation, such as logic and mathematics. People have a tendency to attribute a higher level of intelligence and sagacity to the kinds of animals that have larger cerebral cortices.

There are a number of different approaches to treating anxiety that center on the cortical route. These approaches typically revolve around cognition, which is the mental term for the psychological processes that the vast majority of people refer to as "thinking." Thoughts that originate in the cortex have the potential to either be the cause of anxiety or to have the effect of either increasing or decreasing anxiety levels.

Altering our medicine can help us in certain situations to prevent our mental processes from beginning to contribute to anxiety or from beginning in the first place.

A lesser amount of consideration had been given to the amygdala pathway by anti-anxiety medications up to this time. The amygdala is a relatively small structure, yet despite its size, it contains thousands of distinct cell circuits that are each responsible for a different function. These circuits have an effect on love, sexual behaviour, anger, hostility, and fear. The amygdala's function is to create emotional memories as well as to assign emotional importance to events or things that have occurred in the past. The sentiments and memories associated with those emotions can be either pleasant or negative. In the following discussion, we will focus on the ways in which the amygdala links experiences to feelings of anxiety and creates memories that are anxious-provoking. You will have a better understanding of the amygdala as a result of this, which will make it easier for you to determine how to modify its circuits in order to reduce anxiety.

We humans aren't purposefully aware of the way in which the amygdala connects anxiety to circumstances or things, just as we aren't deliberately aware of the role that the liver plays in digestion. In any event, the emotional programming that occurs in the amygdala has an effect on our behavior. The amygdala is at the very center of where the anxious response is generated, as will be elaborated upon throughout the course of this study. In spite of the fact that the cortex can either initiate or contribute to anxiety, the amygdala is necessary in order to initiate the anxiety response. Because of this, addressing anxiety in a comprehensive manner entails addressing both the cortical circuit and the amygdala pathway simultaneously.

Anxiety and panic attacks, if left untreated, can be extremely frightening experiences that have the potential to radically alter the path that one's life takes. For many people, the memory of their very first panic attack is permanently seared into their minds, leaving them with an enduring impression of terror. It is only natural for you to look for ways to put an end to these bouts of intense fear if you find that you are struggling with them.

Panic attacks plunge the individual into a sudden whirlwind of intense anxiety, often without any discernible cause or imminent threat. Such baseless fears activate the body's emergency response, propelling it into a fight-or-flight mode. It is as if you are under attack, with your body automatically preparing to defend itself against a threat that it believes it is facing.

These episodes don't discriminate; they can afflict anyone, anywhere, catching them off-guard. This unpredictability instills a perpetual fear in victims, making them apprehensive about the next occurrence. As a result, many start to drastically curtail their daily activities, narrowing their world bit by bit, until they're too fearful to even step outside.

Though the peak symptoms of panic attacks are relatively brief for most, they can linger for hours in some. Once they wane, the aftermath often feels like the fatigue from an intense physical exertion. The key to reclaiming your life lies in preempting these attacks. This book will walk you through five powerful strategies that can break the cycle of anxiety, allowing you to take back control of your life.

Being Aware Of The Things That Set Off Your Reactions

Your attachment patterns are activated by circumstances, events, or encounters that are referred collectively as "attachment triggers," which can result in more powerful emotional responses and actions. It is necessary for you to be aware of these triggers in order to understand your attachment style and have a deeper emotional insight into the dynamics of the relationships in your life. In this section, we will discuss the concept of attachment triggers, as well as strategies for successfully recognizing and managing these triggers.

What Exactly Is the Meaning of Attachment Triggers?

Attachment triggers are situations or circumstances that cause an individual to feel emotions that are consistent with their attachment style. Earlier experiences, particularly those from childhood or previous major relationships, are a common source of these triggers. You may have intense feelings of attachment, as well as thoughts and behaviors associated to attachment, when you are presented with attachment triggers.

Common emotional events that encourage attachment

Attachment triggers might look very different from one individual to the next, but here are some of the more typical ones:

The experience of feeling rejected or neglected by a loved one, even if the behavior was unintended or inconsequential, is referred to as perceived rejection.

The feeling that someone significant to you is withdrawing their attention or becoming emotionally distant is a symptom known as perceived abandonment.

Confrontation With Criticism Or Disapproval Confrontation with criticism or disapproval, which can ignite feelings of inadequacy or unworthiness.

When someone does not respond to your needs or emotional cues as you would expect them to, this is an example of lack of responsiveness.

Loss or separation is the experience of being physically or emotionally separated from a loved one, regardless of whether or not the separation is permanent.

Understanding What Sets Off Your Attachment Reactions

Self-awareness is the first step in the process of figuring out what sets off your attachment triggers. The following are some strategies that can assist you in recognizing and identifying your triggers:

Think About How You Reacted Emotionally: Pay close attention to how you feel and how it affects how you respond to different situations, especially those that involve your relationships. Take note of the moments in which you are overcome with powerful feelings such as worry, rage, or despair.

Explore Your Childhood And Past Experiences Think about the experiences you had when you were young and the relationships you had in the past. Consider whether particular occurrences or patterns in your past are connected in any way to the emotional responses you are having right now.

Keep an eye out for recurring patterns: Examine your emotional responses to see if there are any recurring patterns. Do you frequently respond in the same way to particular circumstances or with specific individuals?

Recording Your Triggers in a Journal Keep a log of the events and interactions in your life that bring on particularly powerful feelings or behaviors. Keep a record of the events, your emotions, and the thoughts that were going through your head at the time.

Request Opinions From People Who Can Be Trusted: Discuss your emotional reactions and the causes that set them off with some close friends or a therapist. They might offer insightful advice and remarks that you haven't thought about before or aren't entirely aware of.

How Does Society Play A Role In The Development Of Women's Social Anxiety?

In addition to the socio-environmental elements that we covered before, societal expectations may also be to blame for the elevated levels of social anxiety that are experienced by women. For instance, social anxiety typically develops in adolescence, which is also the time when it often appears to be the most difficult to control. This is because at this point in our lives, we are just starting to develop the kinds of relationships that we believe we will have with us for the rest of our lives. This is also the moment when we have our first awareness of ourselves as "social objects" in the world. At this age, it is also possible to recognize the pressures that exist to seem a certain way, behave a specific way, and adhere to the rules that govern social interactions, whether or not these standards are explicitly stated. When it comes to the pressures that are placed on them by society, it is natural for men to face their own unique set of obstacles. On the other hand, women are subject to a significantly higher level of scrutiny over their social achievement.

In addition to this, many of us start to develop romantic and platonic ties all on our own. This can result in an entirely fresh set of pressures to be "perfect." The proliferation of social media platforms is not to our benefit. Anxiety develops when women are exposed to the "ideals" that society has set and when they attempt to comply to those ideals. Those who choose not to conform to expectations or who are unable to do so typically face greater difficulties than others. It is important to remember, however, that adolescence is a time when the majority of us are still in the process of forming our sense of ourselves. We are unsure of who we are or where we belong in this world.

Neither of these things is clear to us. Because of this, the majority of these challenges can appear to be more difficult at this time.

Impostor syndrome and its relationship to women

The majority of persons who suffer from social anxiety are under the impression that they are unable to do tasks or carry on a discussion effectively. Some people have the mentality that they are not deserving enough to be accepted into a community of people. A significant number of persons who suffer from social anxiety believe that it is only a matter of time until they are "exposed" and mocked. Each and every one of these traits is connected in some way to the imposter syndrome.

The term "impostor syndrome" refers to the sentiments that we have when we mistrust our own traits and skills, as well as when we get the impression that we are trying to pass ourselves off as someone else. People who are afflicted with imposter syndrome have a difficult time believing others when they tell them that they are talented or that they deserve fame, money, or an award. These individuals also have a difficult time accepting compliments. They have a propensity to attribute any success they gain to random occurrences, while also accepting full responsibility for their own faults and failings. Naturally, the vast majority of us have, at some point in our lives, been face to face with this terrifying beast. On the other hand, women are more likely to report having this problem, particularly because they might have to contend with a greater number of doubters and critics on a daily basis.

A survey that was conducted by KPMG not too long ago revealed that seventy-five percent of women executives working in the United States had struggled with imposter syndrome at some point in their careers. (KPMG Study Finds 75% of Executive Women Experience Imposter Syndrome, 2020)

What's more, an astounding 81% say that they need to continually reminding themselves not to fail, but males don't really put as much pressure on themselves. There is no one who is immune to impostor syndrome because if it can affect women who are succeeding in their careers, then it can impact anyone. Because the impostor syndrome keeps us in a constant state of "I'm not good enough," it is difficult for us to be the best versions of ourselves when we are interacting with other people.

Dread of one's own body

The majority of us, when we think of dread, think of physical threats, which are triggered by a known external occurrence, such as a loud noise, peering over the edge of a high location, or standing in front of a crowd of people.

Fear in the body can also manifest itself in the form of phobias, which affect as many as 12% of people at some point in their lives.

Phobias are characterized by an irrational and unreasonable fear of a specific situation, object, or animal. A few examples of common phobias include a fear of spiders, heights, giving speeches in public, and being trapped in small spaces.

When you are experiencing a physiological response to terror, you will notice that your heart is beating faster and that you are taking deeper breaths.

It's possible that you'll get queasy, feel lightheaded, break out in a cold sweat, and have a parched mouth. It's possible that your muscles will feel weaker or more rigid.

The "fight or flight" response that your body has triggered is responsible for all of these events. Without the fear response, you would expose yourself to a significant risk of being harmed.

However, in the environment we live in today, fear can manifest itself in a variety of ways, some of which are more covert than others.

EXTREME ANXIETY

Anxiety can be thought of as a form of prolonged fear. Rather of concentrating on the here and now, it frequently looks to the future.

The United States is seeing an upsurge in the prevalence of anxiety disorders. Every year, the disease affects approximately 18% of the total population.

Anxiety and stress could have effects that linger for a very long time. Cortisol is a hormone that is produced by the body when it is constantly exposed to a stressful environment.

An excess of cortisol can lead to problems sleeping and concentrating, as well as to weight gain and a diminished immune response.

Generalized anxiety can be triggered by taking chances such as starting a new job, allowing ourselves to be vulnerable in a relationship, or even investing our hard-earned money. If you suffer from this condition, you may have trouble falling asleep, be unable to focus, and keep replaying the same scenarios in your head over and over again.

But what really is the central motivation behind these ideas? There are numerous kinds of terror that can get deeply ingrained in the mind.

The Importance Of Technology And Social Media In The Role

The advent of the digital age has brought about an unparalleled level of connectivity as well as chances for self-expression; yet, it has also brought about new obstacles, particularly for adolescents who are struggling with anxiety.

Comparisons Are Made Constantly The platforms for social media often act as highlight reels of other people's life, which can encourage comparisons that are unreasonable. When measured against carefully crafted online personas, some adolescents may experience feelings of inadequacy or anxiety.

Cyberbullying: The digital sphere can be a breeding ground for cyberbullying, as hurtful comments and harassment can intensify an individual's already existing anxieties. Because users remain anonymous online, cyberbullies often feel emboldened to act out.

The worry of missing out on social events or experiences captured online can be a source of anxiety. This dread is referred to as "fear of missing out" (FOMO). It's possible that adolescents will feel the need to continually participate with social media in order to prevent themselves from falling behind.

Detox from Technology: The very technology that contributes to anxiety can also give answers. This concept is known as "digital detox." Teens can be helped to break out from the cycle of comparison and information overload by being encouraged to participate in periodic digital detoxes.

It is essential for both teenagers and the adults who look after them to have a solid understanding of the complexity of social media and technology in relation to anxiety in teenagers. Some of the negative impacts can be mitigated by ensuring that the benefits of connectedness are balanced with thoughtful usage of technology.

It is possible to avoid or stop engaging in excessive thinking, and it is also possible to break the cycle of excessive thinking. To be of assistance to you, please take into consideration the following five suggestions:

1. Make a record of the patterns and the triggers

You might be able to rein in your habit of overthinking with some practice in mindfulness and concentration. You should keep a notebook in which you document specific instances of overthinking or worrying. After some time, patterns will emerge that will assist you in recognizing overthinking triggers when they manifest themselves. You can put this understanding to use to devise a strategy for coping with events that you already know will cause you to engage in excessive thinking.

2. Put your thoughts up for evaluation.

Even if it doesn't feel like it, you shouldn't automatically accept everything that your mind tells you to be true. It is possible to effectively curb excessive thinking by questioning one's worries and rumination by making an effort to take a step back and evaluate them in an objective manner. Determine whether an idea is logical, rational, or helpful by analyzing the data in the scenario and making a decision based on your findings. Naming your overthinking ideas might help you better regulate them, especially if those thoughts aren't useful or don't make sense.

3. Enlist the help of some of your close friends. Do you hear a lot of people telling you that you worry too much or that you think too much? It's highly likely that they're onto something here. Ask a reliable friend to weigh in with their thoughts on the topic that is upsetting you, and tell them to nudge you when you seem stuck in your head.

This will help you become unstuck and find a solution to the problem.

4. Get your body moving as much as you can.

Numerous studies have demonstrated that physical activity can help with a variety of mental health disorders, including anxiety, depression, and others. Overthinking is a chronic condition that can be helped by exercise. Endorphins and other chemicals that make us feel good can be sent to our brains by doing as little as walking around the block for five minutes. The release of your neurological system from the state may also be assisted by engaging in physical activity. It's possible that this will assist you stop dwelling on the traumatic experience you went through.

5. Seek the aid of a specialist. If you feel that your overthinking is taking over more of your life than you would like, you should go to a mental health professional or discuss the issue with

the primary care physician you see. In addition, excessive overthinking can lead to stress, which can contribute to a wide variety of health problems beyond simply mental health issues.

Nevertheless, instances of digestive disorders include physiological symptoms including headaches, fatigue, nausea, and diarrhea. These are all examples of digestive problems.

Having difficulties falling or staying asleep

If you are struggling with overthinking, seeing a therapist or counselor can assist you in acquiring coping techniques that can help you manage rumination. They are also able to assist in identifying and treating any underlying reasons for overthinking, such as worry or depression, which may be contributing to the problem.

Conduct a search of online therapist directories to identify a mental healthcare professional operating in your area.

Effective Counseling

The Counseling Lounge

The QPoC Therapist Directory can be found on Psychology Today.

Gaylesta (a therapist who works with LGBTQ clients), InnoPsych (therapists who work with people of color), and Open Path The Collective Practice of Psychotherapy

Have you arrived at a conclusion after considering a number of different scenarios and the current state of affairs? Are you conscious of the fact that you have a mind that tends to overthink things to the point where your ideas may play out in your head like a looping movie? Do you believe that excessive pondering serves any useful purpose? Even though we are always thinking, we have never given these things much thought in the past.

Taking Control of Your Anxiety in Certain Circumstances

Providing assistance to individuals in conquering their phobias

At some point in our lives, the most of us will, without a doubt, feel the effects of the emotion known as anxiety. It is possible for it to emerge in a variety of ways, and its effects on us can vary depending on the circumstances. Some people are more likely to experience anxiety in social settings, while others may struggle with anxiety brought on by their jobs or certain phobias. In any event, it is essential to have an understanding that anxiety is a normal and natural response to stress, and it is a response that is common.

Nevertheless, anxiety becomes a problem that needs to be handled when it begins to have a negative impact on our day-to-day lives and when it hinders us from performing at our highest potential. In this chapter, we will discuss a variety of strategies for coping with anxiety in a variety of settings and offering people direction toward conquering their phobias and concerns.

Anxiety when in social situations

Many people experience difficulty coping with a common form of anxiety known as social anxiety. It is characterized by an extreme fear of or discomfort in social circumstances, such as meeting new people, giving speeches in public, or attending gatherings. People who suffer from social anxiety disorder frequently have feelings of self-consciousness and concern that they will be criticized or shamed in front of others.

It is imperative that you have the knowledge that there is hope and assistance accessible to you if you, or someone you know, struggles with social anxiety. It is feasible to control social anxiety and feel more comfortable while interacting with others in social settings if one has access to the appropriate assistance and tools.

Exposure therapy is one of the more helpful methods available for overcoming social anxiety. This method entails gradually putting oneself in social circumstances that they fear while simultaneously developing coping mechanisms to handle the symptoms of anxiety. In social circumstances, it may also be beneficial to challenge negative thoughts and beliefs about oneself. Seeking the assistance of a therapist or becoming a member of a support group is another option that can provide helpful tools and direction.

tension caused by one's employment

Although work is an essential component of our lives, it also has the potential to be a major source of stress and anxiety for us. There are several factors that might lead to feelings of anxiety and overload, including demanding workloads, meetings, presentations, and deadlines. Even if some degree of stress at work is to be expected, it is important to be aware of when that stress becomes excessive and begins to have a negative impact on our mental health.

It is essential to place a high priority on self-care in order to effectively handle the stress that is caused by job. This entails taking short breaks throughout the day, establishing clear limits with regard to one's professional duties, and locating and utilizing effective methods for dealing with stress. In addition, acquiring skills in time management can assist in the reduction of stress and the enhancement of productivity. In the event that the stress brought on by one's job becomes intolerable, it may be important to seek the assistance of a mental health expert.

Attacks of sheer panic

Intense bursts of fear or worry can come on quickly and without any warning, and these episodes are known as panic attacks. A rapid heartbeat, shortness of breath, and soreness in the chest are some examples of the physical symptoms that may be present. Attacks of panic can be incapacitating and overwhelming, but it is imperative to keep in mind that they are only transitory and will eventually pass.

Deep breathing exercises are one method that can be used to help manage panic episodes. In order to assist in the regulation of the body's physical response, this requires taking long, steady breaths. The practice of mindfulness practices, such as centering one's attention on the here and now and finding a sense of stability in one's surroundings, may also prove to be beneficial. Going to counseling and learning other ways to deal with stressful situations are both helpful ways to reduce the risk of recurrent panic attacks.

Taking Control of Your Anxiety in Certain Circumstances

Providing assistance to individuals in conquering their phobias

At some point in our lives, the most of us will, without a doubt, feel the effects of the emotion known as anxiety. It is possible for it to emerge in a variety of ways, and its effects on us can vary depending on the circumstances. Some people are more likely to experience anxiety in social settings, while others may struggle with anxiety brought on by their jobs or certain phobias. In any event, it is essential to have an understanding that anxiety is a normal and natural response to stress, and it is a response that is common.

Nevertheless, anxiety becomes a problem that needs to be handled when it begins to have a negative impact on our day-to-day lives and when it hinders us from performing at our highest potential. In this chapter, we will discuss a variety of strategies for coping with anxiety in a variety of settings and offering people direction toward conquering their phobias and concerns.

Anxiety when in social situations

Many people experience difficulty coping with a common form of anxiety known as social anxiety. It is characterized by an extreme fear of or discomfort in social circumstances, such as meeting new people, giving speeches in public, or attending gatherings. People who suffer from social anxiety disorder frequently have feelings of self-consciousness and concern that they will be criticized or shamed in front of others.

It is imperative that you have the knowledge that there is hope and assistance accessible to you if you, or someone you know, struggles with social anxiety. It is feasible to control social anxiety and feel more comfortable while interacting with others in social settings if one has access to the appropriate assistance and tools.

Exposure therapy is one of the more helpful methods available for overcoming social anxiety. This method entails gradually putting oneself in social circumstances that they fear while simultaneously developing coping mechanisms to handle the symptoms of anxiety. In social circumstances, it may also be beneficial to challenge negative thoughts and beliefs about oneself. Seeking the assistance of a therapist or becoming a member of a support group is another option that can provide helpful tools and direction.

tension caused by one's employment

Although work is an essential component of our lives, it also has the potential to be a major source of stress and anxiety for us. There are several factors that might lead to feelings of anxiety and overload, including demanding workloads, meetings, presentations, and deadlines. Even if some degree of stress at work is to be expected, it is important to be aware of when that stress becomes excessive and begins to have a negative impact on our mental health.

It is essential to place a high priority on self-care in order to effectively handle the stress that is caused by job. This entails taking short breaks throughout the day, establishing clear limits with regard to one's professional duties, and locating and utilizing effective methods for dealing with stress. In addition, acquiring skills in time management can assist in the reduction of stress and the enhancement of productivity. In the event that the stress brought on by one's job becomes intolerable, it may be important to seek the assistance of a mental health expert.

Attacks of sheer panic

Intense bursts of fear or worry can come on quickly and without any warning, and these episodes are known as panic attacks. A rapid heartbeat, shortness of breath, and soreness in the chest are some examples of the physical symptoms that may be present. Attacks of panic can be incapacitating and overwhelming, but it is imperative to keep in mind that they are only transitory and will eventually pass.

Deep breathing exercises are one method that can be used to help manage panic episodes. In order to assist in the regulation of the body's physical response, this requires taking long, steady breaths. The practice of mindfulness practices, such as centering one's attention on the here and now and finding a sense of stability in one's surroundings, may also prove to be beneficial. Going to counseling and learning other ways to deal with stressful situations are both helpful ways to reduce the risk of recurrent panic attacks.

Which School Of Thought Within Psychology Best Describes Emotional Intelligence?

Daniel Goleman, a psychologist from the United States, is responsible for the development of the most well-known psychological theory that explains emotional intelligence. It is predicated on the notion that rational intelligence, often known as logical-mathematical intelligence, is not the only type of intellect that can exist. According to the argument put forth by Goleman, logical-mathematical intelligence is insufficient to explain the plethora of mental activity that take place outside of the direct influence of rational thought. Naturally, I am referring to mental states of the emotional variety, such as feelings and emotions, when I say this.

According to the idea proposed by Goleman, emotional intelligence is made up of four primary components: self-awareness, the ability to control one's own emotions, an awareness of the emotions of others, and the ability to manage one's relationships. I would like to go in order, and I would like to begin with self-awareness. It is the capacity to perceive and comprehend one's own feelings, as well as the ability to apply this awareness to the process of decision-making and the management of one's own conduct. It is impossible to empathize with other people if you are unaware of how your own feelings are affecting you. Recognize that you have an emotional side; it is pointless to try to disprove the notion that you are emotionless and callous by any means necessary. We are all human beings, which means that we are all endowed with feelings and passions. That is not something you should be embarrassed about in any way.

On the other side, the ability to regulate one's emotions and communicate one's feelings in a sufficient and appropriate manner is what is meant by the term "emotion management." Many different types of occurrences can be included under the umbrella term of "emotion management." Consider the following illustrations: the capacity to control one's anger in situations when showing anger would be inappropriate; the capacity to control one's melancholy and worry without allowing oneself to be dragged into depression; the capacity to completely enjoy pleasant times when they occur. Take caution not to confuse the act of managing one's emotions with the act of repressing one's feelings! Having emotional control does not imply eradicating feelings entirely from our life; rather, it involves giving them the place and significance that is appropriate for them and recognizing that they have that place.

The third facet of emotional intelligence is known as awareness of others, and it refers to a person's capacity to completely comprehend the emotions that are being experienced by other people. There is no question that none of us are capable of quickly comprehending the mental states of other people. On the other hand, one's awareness of other people can be developed and "trained." If you interact with other people in a way that demonstrates empathy and openness, you will find that you are also capable of understanding the feelings that other people are experiencing. This is an essential component of feeling good about who you are; as I have stated numerous times before, no one can feel good about themselves by turning inward on themselves. Therefore, the importance of this third component of emotional intelligence that Goleman suggested cannot be overstated.

Finally, we come to the management of relationships. It is the capacity to go beyond understanding the feelings of other people and refers to our capacity to develop profound, long-lasting, and meaningful connections with other people. It is comprised of the ability to go beyond understanding the emotions of other people. Although there has been no shortage of criticism over the course of time, there is no denying that the theoretical proposition that Goleman has put up is engaging and fascinating. For instance, there are those who maintain that while IQ can be correctly assessed, the idea of EQ (also known as emotional quotient) is still murky and inadequately established. You are free to entertain your own thoughts regarding the true breadth of this critique. In my opinion, this critique is not nearly as damaging as some others that have been leveled. In the end, even intelligence quotient (IQ) is not nearly as accurate and conclusive a concept as it is sometimes made out to be, as I explained in an earlier chapter of this very same book.

In spite of the fact that Goleman's idea has been called into question, it is now widely accepted that emotional intelligence plays an important part in every person's life. In the following chapter, I will provide a response to an important topic concerning emotional intelligence: why is it so vital for one to feel good about themselves?

Recharge Your Batteries in the Fresh Air

When you're experiencing feelings of being overwhelmed and nervous, it can feel like the walls of your home are closing in on you. Leaving the house and going for a walk is a tried-and-true method for reducing stress and tension almost instantly. The best approach to relieve stress is to get outside and spend some time in nature.

According to a number of studies, spending time outside can have demonstrable health benefits, including a reduction in blood pressure, heart rate, and stress hormones. The natural environment provides an experience that is immersive across multiple senses, engaging not only sight and hearing but also smell, touch, and even taste. You can take your mind off of your worries by doing something relaxing like watching clouds move across the sky or listening to birdsong.

Create a routine in which you spend time outside every day, even if it's just for a few minutes at a time to do things like drink your coffee or walk the dog. You may get both the health advantages of being in nature and exercise by going hiking on any of the nearby paths. Read a book, get some work done, or just eat your dinner outside. Working with your hands provides stress release, which is why gardening and yardwork are such effective stress relievers.

Leave your electronic gadgets inside to get the most out of the experience and fully engage all of your senses. Try out the Japanese practice of forest bathing, which consists of being consciously immersed in the natural world through all of your senses. As you gently travel, pay attention to the different smells, colors, and noises you encounter.

Bring your social group outside to maximize the mood-enhancing advantages of being in the fresh air. Make plans with your friends to participate in activities like outdoor yoga, dinners on the patio, lawn games, and garden clubs. When you go camping, you disconnect from technology and the stimulation of the city.

Make the most of the time you spend outside by tailoring it to your capabilities; even something as simple as sitting on your balcony and watching the birds or lying down in the grass and staring at the clouds can bring some much-needed relief. Sunset strolls give beautiful views that are the perfect way to wind down after a busy day. Find a place with some greenery, whether it's a park, a hiking route, a picnic location, or even your own backyard, and spend some time there. The treatments provided by Mother Nature are only a few steps away.

Now, let's look at some particular strategies to take advantage of the restorative properties of nature: • Go for a walk outside every day for 15 to 30 minutes, but leave your phone inside. Engage all of your sensory faculties.

• Give forest bathing a try by taking a leisurely stroll through a natural setting while paying attention to the sights, sounds, and smells around you.

• Spend some time outside reading a book, listening to music, or simply taking in the sights and sounds of the natural world.

• Take your morning coffee, lunch break, or evening cocktail out into the backyard, onto the balcony, or onto a patio.

Plant a garden outside or go to one of the local botanical gardens. The maintenance and care of plants can be soothing.

• At night, lie down on the grass and look up at the stars while during the day you watch the clouds float by.

• Get some fresh air and exercise outside by going for a walk, riding a bike, going kayaking, or signing up for an outdoor sports league.

- Plan outdoor social gatherings such as dinners on the patio, games on the lawn, or vacations to a campground.

- Find a place to sit close to water, such as a fountain, lake, river, or beach. The sound has a calming effect.

- To feel more connected to the planet and to yourself, try practicing grounding by walking barefoot on grass, soil, or sand.

- Spend your vacation in the great outdoors, whether it be in parks, mountains, cabins, or beach cottages. A change of environment helps you feel refreshed.

- You should throw open the windows in order to let in some natural light and fresh air. Sounds of nature should be played.

Anxiety can be naturally reduced by cultivating a connection to the natural world's inherent calm and expansiveness. Make it a priority to disconnect from technology and spend as much time as you can immersed in the restorative powers of nature. It's right there when you go out the door!

Adjustments to one's way of life, together with support

Modifications to one's way of life and reaching out for assistance are both necessary aspects of successfully managing and conquering social anxiety. These techniques cover a wide range of facets of your day-to-day life, from your physical health to the relationships you maintain with other people, and they have the potential to dramatically improve your general well-being as well as your confidence when you are in social settings.

1. Healthy eating and regular exercise:

There is abundant evidence that points to a relationship between one's physical health and their mental well-being. Making deliberate decisions concerning your eating habits and amount of physical exercise can have a beneficial effect on your mood and anxiety levels:

Diet: It is important to pay attention to the things you eat because different foods might affect your mood as well as your level of anxiety. Include in your diet a variety of fruits, vegetables, lean proteins, whole grains, and healthy fats. A balanced diet is essential to good health. It's possible that certain meals, including those high in omega-3 fatty acids (which may be found in foods like fish, flaxseeds, and walnuts), have particular advantages for mental health.

Regular Physical Activity It has been established that engaging in regular physical activity can lessen feelings of worry and tension. Endorphins, which are natural mood boosters, are the chemicals that are released when you exercise. Exercise should be performed on most days of the week for at least half an hour at a moderate level.

2. Sleep and Social Anxiety: Getting enough quality sleep is absolutely necessary in order to effectively manage social anxiety. If you don't get enough sleep, your anxiety symptoms may become worse, and it may be harder for you to handle social situations.

Hygiene de la sommeil : Create a relaxing nighttime routine, stick to a consistent sleep schedule, and perfect your sleeping environment to get optimal rest. Caffeine and electronic gadgets are two things that should be avoided close to bedtime because they can disrupt sleep.

The Importance of Sleep in Dealing with Anxiety Recognize the correlation between getting enough sleep and feeling less anxious. Maintaining a healthy sleep schedule can assist in mood regulation and boost resiliency in the face of social pressures.

3. Social Support: When it comes to coping with social anxiety, having a support system in place can be really helpful. Your social support network could consist of people you know from work, from school, or even from support groups:

Members of the Family and Friends: Talk about your past experiences and feelings with people you can trust who will listen to you, understand you, and offer you encouragement. If you require it, they are able to provide you with emotional support and go to social events with you.

Support Groups: Participating in a support group for social anxiety might put you in touch with others who are able to empathize with what you are going through. It can be empowering to discuss one's experiences and methods of coping with others in a group setting.

4. Consider Seeking Professional Assistance: When Managing Social Anxiety, You Should Consider Seeking Professional Assistance.

Counseling: therapy Treatments for social anxiety that are based on evidence have shown to be highly helpful. These include cognitive behavioral therapy (CBT), exposure therapy, and other similar treatments. A therapist can offer you direction, methods of coping, and a secure environment in which you may discuss your feelings and the difficulties you are facing.

Medication: In certain instances, a healthcare physician may recommend taking medication that has been prescribed for you in order to ease the symptoms of social anxiety. A thorough treatment strategy may include the use of certain medications, such as those known as selective serotonin reuptake inhibitors (SSRIs).

5. Methods of Stress Reduction: Stress is a typical factor that might bring on feelings of social anxiety. Managing your anxiety more effectively can be accomplished by including tactics that reduce stress into your regular routine:

Meditation and Relaxation: In order to alleviate stress and improve your ability to emotionally regulate yourself, try practicing mindfulness meditation, progressive muscle relaxation, and deep breathing techniques.

Time Management: Make effective use of your time management skills in order to alleviate the stress that is caused by the combination of social obligations and impending deadlines.

Self-Care: Make it a top priority to take care of yourself so that you can keep your mental and emotional health:

A Look at Some Hobbies and Interests: Participate in pursuits that you take pleasure in because doing so can give you a sense of achievement and help you relax.

Setting Boundaries In order to avoid becoming overwhelmed and burned out, it is important to set clear boundaries in both your personal and professional lives.

Be patient with yourself as you work these methods into your routine and keep in mind that making adjustments to your lifestyle will take some time before they start to show significant results. You can effectively manage your social anxiety by building a supportive network and applying these adjustments gradually, which will ultimately lead to increased confidence while interacting with others in social settings.

The Importance Of Self-Care In The Maintenance Of Mental Health

The term "self-care" refers to a collection of behaviors and routines that a person intentionally engages in with the goal of improving his or her mental, emotional, and physical health. It entails providing yourself just a little bit of more love and attention to assist in the management of and relief from the issues that anxiety and depression can bring. In the same way that you may nourish a plant by providing it with water and sunlight, practicing self-care entails nurturing yourself in a variety of different ways in order to build a better and happier state of mind.

Physical, emotional, social, and intellectual self-care are the four main components that comprise what is known as "self-care." When we make deliberate and conscientious attempts to improve these fundamental qualities, we create space for well-being on multiple levels, including the physical, emotional, social, and intellectual. It is important to stress, however, that self-care incorporates all other areas of our well-being, including our financial situation, the state of the environment, and our spiritual life.

It is essential to emphasize that practicing self-care does not entail acting in an egotistical or self-indulgent manner. It is about being aware of your own requirements and making choices on purpose that are beneficial to your overall health and happiness. Practices of self-care can differ significantly from one individual to the next, and what is effective for one person may not be effective for another. The most important thing you can do for your physical, mental, and emotional well-being is to pay attention to yourself, understand what your needs are, and then make decisions that support those needs.

It is impossible to overestimate the significance of practicing good self-care, particularly in the context of overcoming feelings of worry and despair. A look at some of the reasons why taking care of oneself is so important:

Mental and emotional health: Practicing healthy self-care habits can act as a protective barrier for your mind and feelings. Self-care activities assist lower the intensity of unpleasant emotions and symptoms linked with anxiety and depression. These conditions can be reduced in intensity by engaging in self-care activities. It helps you maintain a healthier mental and emotional state by providing you with methods to manage stress, anxiety, and poor mood.

Empowerment and control: Managing mental health conditions like anxiety and depression can frequently leave you feeling powerless or out of control. Self-care gives you the ability to play an active role in your own health and wellness. You are able to restore a sense of control over your life as well as the emotional experiences you have when you make the conscious decision to care for yourself.

Prevention and resiliency: Practicing healthy habits on a consistent basis can act as a buffer against the negative effects of stresses and triggering events. It helps increase resilience, which in turn enables you to recover from challenging circumstances and obstacles in a more expedient manner. The habits that you cultivate via the process of self-care have the potential to build a solid foundation that stops your mental health from deteriorating any further.

Reducing stress is important because long-term stress can make the symptoms of anxiety and depression worse. The physiological effects of stress can be reduced by practicing self-care practices such as deep breathing, meditation, and relaxation exercises. This, in turn, can lead to a state of being that is more tranquil and a state of mind that is more at ease.

Enhanced self-awareness: Participating in activities that promote self-care will inspire you to become more in tune with your own requirements, thoughts, and emotions. This increased self-awareness enables you to recognize triggers, patterns, and early indicators of anxiety or depression, which in turn enables you to intervene and seek treatment before symptoms become more severe.

Enhancement of your physical health: The concept of self-care comprises actions that are beneficial to your physical well-being, such as engaging in regular physical activity, maintaining a healthy diet, and getting enough sleep. Not only does taking care of your body help to maintain your overall health, but it also has a direct and beneficial effect on your mood and the clarity of your thinking.

Quality of life: Practicing healthy self-care habits can help you have more moments of happiness, relaxation, and satisfaction, which all contribute to a higher overall quality of life. Your view on life will improve overall if you participate in pursuits that bring you joy, which in turn will make navigating each day easier and more pleasurable.

Reducing the risk of burnout: When you're struggling with mental health issues like anxiety and depression, it's easy to feel overwhelmed and fatigued all the time. Practicing regular self-care can help prevent burnout by arming you with the tools you need to effectively handle stress and put your own health and happiness first.

Taking care of oneself has a good impact on the way you connect with other people, thus doing so is essential. You are in a better position to engage in meaningful connections and to maintain healthy relationships when you are well rested, emotionally stable, and actively practicing self-compassion.

Long-term well-being: Building a foundation for your long-term well-being by making self-care a regular part of your routine is an important step. It is not enough to simply control the symptoms you are experiencing at the moment; you also need to develop behaviors that will be beneficial to your mental health in the years to come.

Personal development: Practicing good self-care makes it easier to work on one's own development and growth. Your overall sense of identity and sense of self-worth can be bolstered when you participate in activities that present you with new challenges, encourage learning, and give you a sense of accomplishment.

Reduction of self-stigma: Making self-care a priority sends a powerful message to yourself that you are deserving of love, care, and attention, despite of the difficulties you may be experiencing with your mental health. This has the potential to assist in the reduction of negative self-perception and self-stigma.

The practice of self-care is a necessity that provides you with a set of coping mechanisms to help you weather the storms of anxiety and sadness. It gives you the tools you need to fortify your mental and emotional fortitude, improve your general well-being, and play an active role in your journey toward recovery and progress in the process. When you take the time to care for yourself, you not only make an investment in the here and now, but you also lay the groundwork for a more positive and satisfying future for yourself.

Creating And Nurturing Beneficial Relationships

Because we are social animals, the relationships we develop have the potential to have a significant impact on our mental well-being. It's possible that one of the most essential things you can do to help reduce your anxiety is to surround yourself with people who are understanding and sympathetic.

Try to find friends and family members that are understanding and won't pass judgment. Talk to them about how you're feeling, and don't be hesitant to ask for their assistance if you find yourself in a bind. Simply sharing your concerns with a reliable friend could make all the difference in the world in terms of how you feel about them.

If your anxiety is negatively impacting your relationships or your day-to-day life, you should seriously consider getting professional help or visiting support groups.

Mental Clarity and a Detox from Technology

In today's always-connected environment, it's not hard to feel overstimulated by the constant flow of digital information and content. There is some evidence that social media, email, and smartphone use all contribute to heightened levels of anxiety. It's possible that a break from all of your electronic devices will help you restore mental clarity and feel less stressed.

Reduce how much time you spend looking at screens, especially right before night. Stay away from anything that can make you feel uncomfortable or anxious, and think about trying some mindfulness activities so that you can be more present and centered.

You may build a solid foundation for long-term anxiety reduction by incorporating the following five everyday practices into your life: placing a high priority on sleep and nutrition, committing to engaging in regular exercise, establishing supportive friendships, and engaging in a digital detox. Keep in mind that change is a process that takes time, so have patience with yourself as you work to establish and maintain these habits on your way to leading a life that is less fraught with stress and worry.

Variations In Hormone Levels

Because of the delicate interaction that exists between hormones and the chemistry of the brain, hormonal changes can play a significant influence in the development of anxiety in women. These shifts have the potential to throw off the delicate balance of neurotransmitters like serotonin and gamma-aminobutyric acid (GABA), both of which play an important role in maintaining a stable mood and reducing anxiety. The following are some of the ways that fluctuating hormone levels can lead to anxiety in women:

1. The Cycle of Menstruation: Mood can be affected by fluctuations in hormone levels that occur during the menstrual cycle, particularly in the days preceding up to menstruation. The decline in estrogen and progesterone levels that occurs immediately prior to a woman's

period can cause symptoms that are grouped together and referred to as premenstrual syndrome (PMS). Some women experience heightened anxiety, irritability, and mood fluctuations as a result of their premenstrual syndrome (PMS).

2. Premenstrual dysphoric disorder (PMDD), sometimes known as premenstrual blues PMDD is a severe type of PMS that manifests itself in the days leading up to menstruation with a wide range of incapacitating mental and physical symptoms. Women who suffer from premenstrual dysphoric disorder (PMDD) may experience severe anxiety, in addition to depression, irritability, and hostility.

3. Pregnancy: The major hormonal shifts that occur during pregnancy can have an effect on the neurotransmitters already present in the brain. Some pregnant women struggle with anxiety, which is typically brought on by worries about the well-being of their unborn child, the forthcoming adjustments in their lives,

or the physical aches and pains that are common during pregnancy.

4. The Postpartum Period: Following delivery of a child, a woman's hormone levels continue to fluctuate, particularly seeing a sharp decline in estrogen and progesterone levels. This can put a woman at risk for postpartum mental disorders, such as postpartum anxiety.

Some first-time mothers have an abnormally high level of anxiety regarding the health of their infants or their capacity to properly care for their children.

5. Menopause: The change from reproductive years to post-menopausal years is accompanied by a drop in estrogen levels. The hormone estrogen has been demonstrated to have a protective influence on the regulation of mood, and a drop in estrogen has been linked to mood fluctuations as well as an increased risk of developing anxiety and depression. During menopause, some

women report feeling considerable levels of anxiety.

6. Hormones Produced by the Thyroid Thyroid hormones, which are responsible for regulating metabolism and energy levels, can also have an effect on mood. Symptoms of anxiety, as well as depression and other mood disorders, can be brought on by a thyroid that is either overactive (hyperthyroidism) or underactive (hypothyroidism).

7. Mood abnormalities Associated with Hormonal Contraceptives The use of hormonal contraceptives, such as birth control tablets, has been linked to mood abnormalities in some women. One of these changes may be an elevated level of anxiousness. It is essential to keep in mind that this does not happen to all women, and that women's reactions to hormonal birth control pills can vary greatly.

8. Hormone Replacement Therapy (HRT): In order to reduce the symptoms of menopause, a doctor may recommend

hormone replacement therapy to women who are going through the transition. However, hormone replacement therapy can also have an effect on a person's mood as well as their level of anxiety.

These changes in hormone levels have an effect on the chemistry of the brain because they alter the levels of neurotransmitters as well as their activity. For instance, estrogen and progesterone both have neuroprotective qualities and can increase the availability of serotonin and GABA, two neurotransmitters that are known to have a sedative and mood-balancing impact. Mood swings and an increased susceptibility to anxiety can be the result of fluctuations in hormone levels, which can upset the equilibrium of these neurotransmitters and cause these levels to be affected.

It is critical to understand that hormonal changes, which might play a role in the development of anxiety in women, are not the only cause of the condition.

Anxiety is a complex disorder that can be caused by a number of different things, including a person's genetics, the stressors in their surroundings, and their own personal experiences in life. In addition, not all women will experience anxiety as a direct result of changes in their hormone levels, and some women may be more resistant to the effects of these shifts.

If a woman notices that her mental health and well-being are adversely impacted by hormone variations, she should seek support from healthcare professionals or mental health practitioners. Alterations to one's lifestyle, psychotherapy, medicine, and coping mechanisms that can be used to handle anxiety during periods of hormonal transition are all potential treatment choices.

Benefits Of Positive Affirmations For Those Struggling With Sleep Anxiety

Affirmations of positivity work to alleviate tension and anxiety by shifting your attention away from negative ideas and toward more upbeat and optimistic ones. You can lessen the stress and anxiety connected with sleep by calming your thoughts, reducing stress, and repeating positive affirmations such as "I am calm and relaxed."

Improving Your Self-Belief and Confidence Improving your self-belief and confidence in your ability to fall asleep is a common solution for people who struggle with sleep anxiety. Affirmations like "I am capable of falling asleep easily" or "I trust my body's ability to find restful sleep" might help you feel more confident in yourself and reinforce the positive thoughts you already have about your ability to sleep well.

Affirmations are another tool that can be utilized in the process of establishing a favorable atmosphere for sleep. You can turn your physical area into an environment that is conducive to relaxation and sleep by using affirmations such as "My bedroom is a peaceful sanctuary for sleep" or "I create a soothing bedtime routine."

Several Useful Suggestions to Help You Integrate Positive Affirmations Into Your Everyday Life

Pick affirmations that are pertinent: Choose affirmations that speak to the specific anxieties you have with your sleep and go with those. Consider the ideas or beliefs that are making it difficult for you to get to sleep, and then formulate affirmations that will help you overcome those issues. For instance, if you frequently fear that you won't be able to go asleep, repeating an affirmation to yourself such as "I easily drift into deep and restful sleep" can be useful.

Repetition and consistency: Throughout the day, make a habit of repeating your chosen positive affirmations to yourself. Dedicate specific periods of the day, such as the morning and the evening, to the practice of repeating these phrases to yourself. Repetition is essential if you want to successfully implant these constructive beliefs deep within your subconscious mind.

Visual cues and reminders: Post written affirmations in places where they will be seen, such as on the wall of your bedroom, the mirror in your bathroom, or the lock screen of your phone. You may maintain your affirmations at the forefront of your mind by using these visual cues as reminders to reinforce positive thoughts and keep them in the forefront of your mind.

Emotional connection: When you are saying your affirmations, you should make an effort to conjure up the feelings that are connected to the positive remarks. As you repeat these affirmations to yourself, picture yourself in a state of peacefulness, complete relaxation, and restful slumber. The effect that your affirmations have on your subconscious mind can be strengthened by connecting them to emotions.

Affirmations to say before bed: Make the practice of saying affirmations before bed part of your regular habit. While you are winding down for the night, repeat sleep-related affirmations to yourself. This will allow you to relax and get ready for a restful night's sleep. This routine helps you redirect your attention away from anxious thoughts and encourages a more optimistic mentality just before bedtime.

Affirmations of a positive nature have the capacity to alter your perspective and relieve the anxiety that can prevent sleep. You can create a positive mindset and conquer sleep anxiety if you have a grasp of the concept of positive affirmations, recognition of the advantages of positive affirmations for sleep anxiety, and implementation of practical techniques for incorporating positive affirmations into your everyday life.

Acknowledge the power of positive affirmations and set off on a path to more restful and revitalizing sleep.

Aspects Of The Natural World

1. The manner in which parents interact with their children can have an effect on the child's propensity to suffer from social anxiety later in life. Parenting approaches that are overprotective or too critical might contribute to a child's insecurity as well as their fear of being judged by their peers.

2. Relationships with Peers: Unfavorable interactions with one's contemporaries, such as being bullied or being rejected, can be a factor in the development of social anxiety. Children who suffer persistent social issues or who are isolated from their peers may internalize these experiences and develop increased social anxiety as a result.

3. Children are like sponges in that they pick up behaviors from their

environment. This is referred to as social learning. They may unknowingly pick up on these signs if they observe their parents or caregivers engaging in nervous behaviors or avoiding social situations as if it were a well-rehearsed magic show. It's very similar to picking up dance moves by watching others around you and imitating their flawless movements. They are gradually becoming actors in the same worried performance as they replicate these actions, which is as if they are creating their own mask of social anxiety in the process of mirroring what they have observed and imitating what they have seen.

Previous Upsetting Events and Experiences

1. Trauma and Bullying: Children who have been through traumatic experiences, such as bullying, physical or emotional abuse, or uncomfortable social circumstances, have a higher risk of developing social anxiety as a kind of self-protection. These memories from

the past can give rise to a profound dread of experiencing something comparable in the future.

Imagine that a child's self-esteem is a delicate vase, and that a single experience of being humiliated or rejected in a social setting is the moment when it shatters into pieces. This is what may happen to a child's self-esteem when they go through these types of situations. This life-changing occurrence can be compared to a break in a vase that never quite heals completely and leaves behind a lingering impression. It's like having an emotional scar that constantly brings up sad memories of that time in your life. This fear, like a shadow, might linger over the child's future social contacts, forcing them to try evasive maneuvers in order to escape the risk of recreating an ordeal similar to the one they had in the past. It's as though they've realized the importance of being careful so as to avoid breaking their fragile emotional vase even further.

3. Receiving Early Negative criticism
Children are extremely sensitive to the criticism they receive from their caretakers as well as from their peers. Children can develop social anxiety and lose their self-confidence if they are given repeated criticism or negative comments regarding their interactions with other people.

It is essential to get an understanding of the factors that contribute to children's social anxiety if one want to properly address and treat the disease. It is essential to understand that social anxiety is rarely caused by just one thing, but rather, is frequently the consequence of a confluence of factors, including a genetic predisposition, contextual influences, and previous experiences. In the following chapters, we will discuss many tactics and interventions that, regardless of the underlying causes of social anxiety, can assist youngsters in overcoming the effects of their condition.

Illustrations From Everyday Life

Acquiring knowledge of the cognitive triangle is not limited to the realm of academia; rather, it has practical applications that can make a significant contribution to one's quality of life. Let's get away from the clinical atmosphere of a therapist's office and talk about some real-life circumstances instead of dwelling on the theoretical. These real-world examples can provide you with both the vocabulary and the context to recognize patterns, making it possible for you to use the cognitive triangle as a tool for self-regulation.

First, there's the proverbial "bad day" at the office.

Imagine that you've had a difficult day at work, when you were criticized by your manager and a project didn't turn out the way it was supposed to. You could be having the notion, "I'm not good enough for this job." The very concept of it brings on thoughts of inadequacy as well as melancholy. Because of this, your conduct may consist of avoiding your coworkers and withdrawing inside your office, which will only serve to further perpetuate the notion that you are an unreliable and isolated individual. The triangle is currently stuck in a pathological loop. If you are able to recognize the pattern, however, you will have the ability to interfere at any point in the process. This may involve disputing the first concept that comes to mind or engaging in other constructive behaviors such as asking for feedback.

Scenario 2: Jealousy Caused by Social Media

As you go through social media, you come across posts by friends and acquaintances in which they share photographs of their trips, their picture-perfect families, or their most recent professional achievements. The question "Why is everyone doing better than me?" starts to cross your mind. This results in sentiments of envy and discontentment in the individual. As a consequence of this, it is possible that you will withdraw from social activities or perhaps behave irritably toward other people. But if you can catch yourself having that first idea, you have the ability to adjust the emotional response you have to the images, possibly by re-contextualizing them as snapshots rather than as complete narrative. By doing so, your conduct will follow suit, perhaps by centering on thankfulness for what you already own, which will result in a more emotionally balanced state of being for you.

Scenario 3: Standing in Line at the Grocery Store

You're running late, and the line at the supermarket is really lengthy. The thought that runs through your head is, "This is going to take forever, and I don't have time for this." This thinking has the potential to induce feelings of impatience and anger, both of which can lead to irritable behavior, such as heaving loud sighs or staring angrily at the cashier. Once again, there has never been a better opportunity to step in. Would it be possible for you to question your idea and replace it with the phrase, "This is an opportunity to slow down and breathe," thereby influencing your emotional response as well as your behavior?

The most important thing to take away from this is the realization that even the most routine aspects of daily life present many possibilities to apply the cognitive triangle. You'll be able to feel more in control of the situation once you've identified these specific instances. It is often the case that the smallest adjustments will, in the long run, result in the most substantial shift. Keep this triangle in mind as you go about your day and make your way through the many activities. Each vertex—whether it be a thought, an emotion, or a behavior—represents a door you may go through or a knob you can turn in order to completely change the overall layout of your psychological experience.

Keep in mind that you don't have to completely reorganize your thought process in a single night. Changes that are even relatively insignificant can snowball into significant ones. Keep the cognitive triangle in mind the next time you find yourself mired in an emotional muck and think about how you got there. It's possible that the first step on your journey to better self-awareness and control is something as basic as making a mental note of the ways in which your day-to-day activities are connected to one another.

The second exercise is titled "What's It to You?"

One of the most widespread forms of cognitive distortion is the practice of excessive personalisation. Taking things personally and placing the responsibility on ourselves is a simpler alternative to objectively examining a situation; yet, doing so puts us in a more precarious position. When you have a tendency to personalize things, you only see them from a limited perspective, which makes it difficult to enjoy life to the extent that you should. Because of these factors, you need to acquire the skill of avoiding personalizing.

How are you able to prevent yourself from taking things personally? The first thing you need to do is become conscious of the many occasions on which you blame yourself for things that have happened. Do you believe it is your responsibility if a best friend of yours fails to show up for a scheduled appointment with you at the last minute? When you've been ill, have you ever tried to find reasons to blame yourself? If the answer to both of these questions is "yes," then you have a propensity to make things more personal. The question "do you have some sort of control or responsibility over them?" is the most effective approach to differentiate between events that occur because of you and those that do not, because it allows you to determine which ones are caused by you and which ones are not. You shouldn't put the burden on yourself because you can't control whether or not your closest friend is available or your physical health. Consider the steps you may take to improve the circumstance each time you find yourself unsure of whether or not you are engaging in personalization. If you are unable to take any action, you cannot be held responsible or in charge of the situation. Taking things personally in general, but in relationships in particular, is a poor strategy because you can't always know the reasons why people do the things they do. There are occasions when people are merely unaware of the behaviors or thoughts that they are engaging in. It serves no use, then, to accept responsibility for the actions of others. Because you can never know all that goes on in the lives and brains of other people, you can never be accountable for the things they do. Take charge of the aspects of your life that are in your power to improve it and learn to let go of the rest if you want to lead a life that is full of joy and contentment.

Foods That Are Good For Your Mental Health

Now, let's have a look at some of the meals that, in the fight against anxiety, could prove to be your best allies:

1. Fruits and vegetables: These foods are rich in the vitamins, minerals, and fiber that are essential to the health of both your body and the microorganisms that live in your gut. Aim for a platter that is vibrant and filled with enough of them.

2. Foods Containing Whole Grains: Cereals like brown rice, bread made with whole wheat, and oats are excellent sources of sustained energy and promote intestinal health.

3. Lean Proteins: Chicken, fish, legumes, and tofu are all wonderful sources of protein that do not include the high levels of saturated fat that are found in processed meats.

4. Nutrients Rich in Healthful Fats: Avocados, almonds, and olive oil are all excellent sources of the healthy fats that are beneficial to brain function and that help to reduce inflammation.

5. Probiotics: Yogurt and fermented foods like kimchi and sauerkraut contain helpful bacteria that can enhance gut health and are found in probiotics.

6. Keeping hydrated: Water is an essential component of a healthy body, including a healthy mind. Your state of mind as well as your level of energy might be impacted by dehydration.

Imagine that you start the day with a bowl of oatmeal that is topped with berries, that for lunch you have a salad with grilled chicken on it, and that for your snack you have some nuts and an apple. You cook the fish in the oven and serve it with steamed broccoli and brown rice for dinner. You drink water to keep yourself hydrated all throughout the day. The gut-brain link is supported by this type of diet, which may also help lessen feelings of worry.

To put it another way, everything you put in your body has an effect not just on your body but also on your mind. Your gut health can have a positive affect on your mood, and eating foods that support gut health can help lower anxiety. Therefore, you should look of each meal as an opportunity to nourish not only your gut but also your mental well-being.

Anxiety and Loss of Sleep

You can think of sleep as your body's way of handling stress and recharging its batteries at the same time. Establishing Healthy Sleep Habits and Addressing Sleep Disorders are the Two key components of Sleep and Anxiety That We Will discuss in This Section In this section, we will discuss two key components of sleep and anxiety. These insights, which are expressed in simple terms, will assist you in getting a more peaceful night's sleep and lowering your levels of worry.

Developing Beneficial Patterns of Sleeping

Imagine that your body is a complex and intricate piece of machinery. In the same way that machines require routine maintenance, the human body requires healthy sleeping patterns in order to perform at its best. Having good sleep hygiene is like to having a well-oiled engine that operates without any hiccups.

The following is a guide to developing good sleeping patterns:

1. Maintain a Regular Schedule Make it a goal to go to bed and get up at the same time every day, including on the

weekends. This helps to keep the internal clock of your body in check.

2. Establish a relaxing Bedtime Routine Before turning in for the night, try engaging in some relaxing activities such as reading, doing some gentle stretches, or taking some deep breaths. Stay away from anything that could get your blood pumping, like watching an action movie.

3. Make Sure Your Sleep Environment Is Comfortable: Ensure that your sleeping place is cozy. This includes a temperature that is pleasant, a comfy mattress, and as little light and noise as possible in the room.

4. Reduce the amount of time spent in front of electronic devices. The blue light emitted by electronic devices can prevent your body from producing melatonin, a hormone that assists with sleep. At least one hour before going to bed, you should stay away from screens.

5. Be Aware of What You Put in Your Body: Large meals, coffee, and alcohol

should not be consumed within a few hours of going to bed. These things can make sleeping difficult.

Take, for instance, the scenario in which you decide that you will go to bed at 10:00 PM and wake up at 6:00 AM every day. Before you go to sleep, you spend half an hour reading a book, you make sure your room is dark and quiet, and you don't drink any coffee after midnight. These routines teach your body to identify when it is time to sleep, which makes it much simpler to get to sleep and to remain asleep throughout the night.

Additional Methods Of Caring For Oneself

5. Mindful Breathing: Make it a part of your everyday routine to practice mindfulness by engaging in deep breathing exercises. You can better manage stress and stay grounded with the help of this technique.

6. Maintain a healthy diet by paying attention to the foods you eat and selecting options that are beneficial to both your physical and mental health. Your mental health can be significantly improved by eating foods that are nutritious and in appropriate proportions.

7. Engage in Regular Physical Activity: It is well known that engaging in regular physical activity will help boost mood and release endorphins. A difference can be made by taking even a brief stroll every day.

8. If you want quality sleep, make proper sleep hygiene a top priority. It is essential to your mental and emotional health that you receive adequate restorative sleep, so make sure you get plenty of it.

9. Connection: Invest in the ties you have and look to your family and friends for emotional support. The ability to connect with others and get support from others is critical to one's mental health.

10. Eliminate Potential Stressors: Recognize and Take Control of the Stressors in Your Life. To alleviate stress in your life, establish boundaries, learn to delegate responsibilities, and improve your time management skills.

11. Practice Consciousness-Raising Meditation Do your best to incorporate attentive meditation into your everyday routine. Being mindful can assist you in remaining in the here and now, in better managing negative thoughts, and in experiencing less worry.

12. Develop an attitude of thankfulness by keeping a daily gratitude journal in which you write down a few things for which you are thankful. This practice has the potential to reorient your attention toward more positive things.

13. Engage in Creative Activities That Bring You delight 13. Whether it's art, music, writing, or any other kind of self-expression, you should engage in creative activities that bring you delight.

14. Don't Hesitate to Seek expert Assistance If you are having difficulties with your mental or emotional health, don't be afraid to seek assistance from a mental health expert.

You can build a holistic approach to the maintenance of your emotional and mental wellness by including these self-care practices into your daily routine, along with the reading of scripture and prayer. By adhering to these practices on a consistent basis, you can build a solid foundation for resilience and inner serenity, which will assist you in navigating the obstacles of life with grace and power.

Methods That Can Help Improve One's Social Abilities

1. Establish Precise Objectives: To get started, you need to be clear about which of your social skills you want to improve. Clear goals will serve as your compass, pointing you in the right direction whether you're trying to improve your eye contact, hone your active listening abilities, or cultivate a sense of ease in social settings.

2. Ask for comments Don't be afraid to ask for comments from someone you know you can trust, such as family members, friends, or coworkers. They are able to provide helpful insights into your social capabilities as well as areas in which you could improve.

3. Practice, Practice, and More Practice: Improving social skills is similar to learning a new language or playing a musical instrument; it requires regular *practice in order to be successful. Participating actively in social circumstances that test your boundaries and progressively widening your comfort zone are both excellent ways to give yourself a challenge.*

4. Watch People Who Have Good Social Skills and Learn From Them Identify people who have good social skills and watch how they interact with others. You can "stand on the shoulders of those who excelled in this art" by learning from those who came before you, adapting their methods, and incorporating those methods into your own style.

5. Think About Getting Professional Help If your life is significantly impacted by social anxiety or a particular social issue, you might think about getting guidance from a therapist or counselor. They are able to offer individualized strategies, support, and a secure environment to help individuals navigate and prevail over these challenges.

6. Participate Actively in Social Groups Taking part in activities such as clubs, organizations, or programs that are matched with your interests is a wonderful approach to hone your social skills in an atmosphere that is both structured and encouraging.

7. Evaluate your progress on a regular basis and be open to modify your strategy in response to the findings of these evaluations. Keep in mind that improving your social skills is a journey that never ends, and that personal development necessitates adaptability and flexibility.

The Path To Serenity: Recognizing The Importance Of Mindfulness

As women, we frequently discover that, as we move through the intricate dance that is life, we are swaying to the complicated rhythms of a multitude of roles, expectations, and duties. The ups and downs that are inevitable in life can sometimes turn into a cacophony of tension, pressure, and anxiety for those living through it. However, hidden inside this cacophonous symphony is a tune of mindfulness that can lead us to a place of calm and equilibrium; a tune of peace and tranquility that can be found within the midst of the mayhem.

The practice of mindfulness is analogous to hearing a soft whisper amidst the cacophony, or a bright beacon of light in the gloom, directing us to firmly plant ourselves in the here and now and discover comfort in the present moment. It is a path to transforming the shadows of worry about the unknown future into the golden brightness of the present moment, and it is a journey to creating a garden of optimistic ideas. Because we learn to notice our own thoughts and feelings without passing judgment on them as we practice embracing the core of each moment, we are able to construct a tapestry of optimism and hope, thereby reducing the shadows cast by fear.

The embrace of mindfulness is not merely a mental hug; rather, it is an embrace that encompasses the whole person, calming the bodily echoes of tension that vibrate through our bodies. The bodily signs of stress, such as a racing heartbeat, tremors, and beads of sweat, can be overpowering, which can turn the tiniest whispers of worry into thunderous roars of anxiety. Mindfulness, which involves paying attention to one's breathing and finding ways to relax, acts as a salve for these physical echoes, like a lullaby that soothes and calms the roiling seas within us.

When we begin the journey of mindfulness, it is as if we are opening a window to our souls. This provides us with the opportunity to examine our thoughts, feelings, and triggers with greater clarity and comprehension. It is a journey of self-discovery that enables us to identify the circumstances and choices that are the primary contributors to our anxious feelings. When we are able to recognize these catalysts, it is as if we had a map of our minds. This gives us the ability to travel through our thoughts and feelings, as well as to prepare for and manage our responses to anxiety triggers.

The practice of mindfulness is not only a means to loving and accepting oneself, but also a technique to start treating oneself with the same kindness and compassion that is typically reserved for dealing with other people. Anxiety's shadows are frequently tinged with guilt and shame, which can make us feel as though we are being held captive within our own brains. Mindfulness training, on the other hand, is analogous to a key that can unlock these restraints and free us to accept our authentic selves, to shower ourselves with love and acceptance, to lessen the burden of anxiety, and to improve our mental and emotional well-being.

The act of incorporating mindfulness into our day-to-day lives is analogous to knitting together strands of tranquility and equilibrium into our life. The countless practices of mindfulness, such as meditating, practicing deep breathing, or performing body scans, are like diverse shades of calmness that we might use to paint our life with. Discovering the ideal tone and incorporating it into our day-to-day lives is of the utmost importance. The practice of mindfulness on a consistent basis can assist us in creating a life that is harmonious, balanced, and full of satisfaction for ourselves and others around us.

In this chapter, we are going to take a stroll together through the peaceful pathways of mindfulness, discovering the many nuances of tranquility and gaining a knowledge of how to incorporate them into our everyday lives. Let's get started on our trip to tranquility, where we will search for the tune of calm amidst the symphony of life, and where we will move to the rhythms of mindfulness, embracing each moment with love, acceptance, and delight.

Anxiety Disorders Can Take Many Forms.

Anxiety has a wide range of effects on different people, leading to a diverse set of difficulties.

The most common form of anxiety condition is known as generalized anxiety disorder, or GAD. People who suffer with GAD have intense anxiety and concern over a wide variety of situations and occurrences in their lives.

They have difficulty controlling their anxiety and concern, which is accompanied by restlessness and a constant feeling of "being revved up or on edge." People in this situation are not nervous about anything in particular, and there is no obvious basis for their anxiety.

Substance abuse: People who are heavy users of drugs, alcohol, or other substances often struggle with anxiety as the effects of the substance begin to wear off (this process is known as withdrawal).

Personality traits can have a role in the development of anxiety-related diseases. For example, people who strive for perfection or who have a strong desire to take the lead are more likely to struggle with these conditions.

Anxiety disorders of a certain kind

Anxiety has a wide range of effects on different people, leading to a diverse set of difficulties.

The most common types of anxiety disorders are as follows: Generalized Anxiety Disorder (GAD) People who suffer from GAD have excessive anxiety and concern over a variety of different occurrences and scenarios. They have difficulty controlling their feelings of worry and anxiety, which is accompanied by restlessness and a constant sense of "being revved up or on edge." People in this situation are not nervous about anything in particular, and there is no obvious basis for their anxiety.

The acronym OCD stands for obsessive-compulsive disorder. OCD sufferers experience persistent thoughts and worries, which can lead to feelings of worry. They alleviate their anxiety by performing certain actions in a pattern over and over again.

For instance, a person who has a phobia of germs and pollution may repeatedly wash their hands and the vessels in their home because they are afraid of getting sick from them.

Phobia de l'espace public et troubles liés à l'anxiétésociale People who suffer from social anxiety disorder experience intense fear whenever they are forced into social or performance-related situations in which they may be observed by others.

They are paralyzed with the fear that anything they do or say could bring shame or dishonor upon them. They have no self-confidence.

These individuals are incapable of handling even the most basic of tasks, such as making polite conversation or eating in public.

Fears that are more specific Phobias are irrational fears, and people who suffer from them will go to great lengths to steer clear of the object of their dread or the situation that makes them uncomfortable.

Their anxieties may range from seemingly benign things like spiders and high-rise buildings to more outlandish situations like flying in an airplane or being in a crowded area.

The acronym PTSD stands for post-traumatic stress disorder. The development of post-traumatic stress disorder (PTSD) is a possibility for those who have experienced or seen a traumatic event, such as an accident or an assault.

The individual will have trouble falling asleep and will find it difficult to relax as a result of the continuous memories of the occurrence.

I suffer from panic disorder. People who have panic disorder experience panic attacks that are out of their control and are accompanied by a variety of unpleasant physical symptoms. These symptoms can include feeling faint, having difficulty breathing, and heavy perspiration.

Patients also report experiencing psychological symptoms (thoughts) during these times, including a feeling of impending doom and sensations such as 'I am about to die' or 'I shall go insane.' During these times, patients say they have thoughts like these.

These attacks take place for no discernible reason, and the victim consequently lives in constant fear of being subjected to yet another incident of the same kind.

I suffer from panic disorder. People who have panic disorder experience panic attacks that are out of their control and are accompanied by a variety of unpleasant physical symptoms. These symptoms can include feeling faint, having difficulty breathing, and heavy perspiration. During these times, patients also describe psychological symptoms (thoughts), including a sense of impending doom and sensations such as "I am going to die" or "I shall go crazy." These assaults occur for no apparent reason, and the victim consequently lives in continual terror of experiencing another episode of the same kind.

Getting treatment for anxiety problems through therapy

Anxiety disorders can be conquered, but it is important to remember that the severity of the disease should not be underestimated.

It is strongly recommended that you seek the advice and treatment of a qualified professional if you experience any of the symptoms described above. Treatment for anxiety disorders may involve medication, talk therapy, or a combination of the two.

Providing care for a person who suffers from anxiety disorders

If you are a What distinguishes normal anxiety from an anxiety disorder is the severity of the symptoms.

You can use this quick checklist to determine whether or not you have an anxiety problem by considering the following items:

A constant state of unease

Worrying about things like one's finances, upcoming job interviews or tests, or other significant upcoming events.

The feeling of having "butterflies in your stomach" before giving a speech in front of a large audience or participating in a major conference.

A fear of something that could potentially cause harm, such as a stray dog that barks at you when you're walking down the street.

Concern or melancholy experienced in the immediate aftermath of a traumatic event, such as the loss of a loved one.

Upkeep of personal cleanliness as well as that of one's immediate environment.

Starting to perspire just before a very important competition.

Disorders related to anxiety

When you worry constantly and excessively for no apparent reason, it makes it more difficult for you to complete the activities of daily living.

A fear of participating in any social or performance-related activities because of the potential for receiving negative feedback from other people in those situations. You are concerned that you will act in a manner that will bring shame or embarrassment to yourself or others.

irrational dread of a thing or place, such as the anxiety that comes from entering an elevator due to the mistaken belief that there is no way out.

After being exposed to a severely traumatic event in the past, the individual may experience recurring flashbacks, nightmares, and subsequent concern as a result.

Conducting compulsive and repetitive acts of cleaning and rearranging the items and objects in your immediate environment.

recurring panic attacks that are accompanied by tense feelings such as "I am going to die" for no apparent reason, as well as the constant dread of having another attack.

Challenges To Communication In Relationships Caused By Attention Deficit Hyperactivity Disorder

Having the ability to communicate clearly and effectively is essential to maintaining a successful relationship; however, ADHD can create challenges that make this task more difficult.

Obstacles to Effective Communication: - Difficulty Maintaining Attention During Conversations People who have ADHD may have trouble maintaining their attention during conversations, which can result in numerous interruptions and an inability to fully participate in the topic.

- Impulsivity and Interruptions: The irresponsibility that is linked with ADHD can manifest itself as pauses during conversations, which slows the flow of communication and causes annoyance for both parties.

- Forgetfulness and Inconsistency: ADHD can cause forgetfulness, which can make it difficult to remember conversations, plans, or deals. This can have a negative impact on trust and reliability, both of which are important for effective communication.

3. The Relationship Between the Physcial Aspects of Intimacy and ADHD

ADHD can also have an impact on a couple's ability to be physically near, which is an essential component of any loving relationship.

Influence on Sexual and Physical Intimacy: Inattention during Intimate Moments: Difficulty in keeping attention can influence the quality and length of intimate moments, leaving both couples feeling unsatisfied as a result. Inattention can be caused by either partner being preoccupied with other things throughout the time.

- Hyperactivity: People with ADHD who experience restlessness may find it difficult to remain calm and focused even when they are in close physical proximity to another person, which might hinder their ability to form a connection with that person.

- Impulsivity in Physical behaviorsThe impulsivity that is associated with ADHD can lead to behaviors that are performed on the spur of the moment during private moments, which can cause discomfort or misunderstanding between partners.

The Acronym "Cbt" Stands For Cognitive Behavioral Therapy.

Cognitive Behavioral Therapy, also known simply as CBT, is a method that has been demonstrated to be useful in the treatment of a wide variety of mental health issues, including anxiety. Individuals can ease their anxiety and enhance their general well-being by detecting and changing negative thinking patterns and behaviors, which is the central tenet of cognitive behavioral therapy (CBT), which is founded on the hypothesis that our thoughts, feelings, and behaviors are interconnected. Let's delve further into cognitive behavioral therapy (CBT) as an anxiety management tool:

Having an understanding of CBT:

- Cognitive behavioral therapy, or CBT, is a psychotherapy approach that is evidence-based, follows a structured format, and focuses on modifying maladaptive thought patterns and behaviors related with anxiety.

- It is commonly thought of as a form of goal-oriented therapy that may be completed in a very short period of time, typically running from 12 to 16 sessions, but the duration might vary depending on the specific requirements of the patient.

Participatory and Dedicated to Achieving Goals:

- Cognitive behavioral therapy (CBT) is a process that involves collaboration between the individual seeking treatment and the therapist. They collaborate in order to establish clear and attainable objectives for the therapy.

- Reducing anxiety symptoms, determining the causes of the anxiety, and creating healthy coping mechanisms are frequently included in these objectives.

Recognizing Automatic Negative thinking Patterns That Contribute to Anxiety: Cognitive behavioral therapy (CBT) assists individuals in recognizing automatic negative thinking patterns that contribute to anxiety. These thoughts frequently involve considering the worst case scenario, worrying an excessive amount, and engaging in cognitive distortions.

Irrational thought processes are known as cognitive distortions. Some examples of cognitive distortions include all-or-nothing thinking, overgeneralization, and mind reading. Individuals learn how to confront and reframe their distorted thinking through the use of CBT.

Behavioral Experiments: - Cognitive Behavioral Therapy (CBT) encourages individuals to examine the validity of their worried ideas by participating in behavioral experiments. For someone who has a phobia of public speaking, for instance, confronting their anxiety can involve progressively increasing the amount of time they spend speaking in front of others.

Exposure and Response Prevention (ERP) is a specialized kind of cognitive behavioral therapy (CBT) that is frequently utilized in the treatment of anxiety disorders, such as obsessive-compulsive disorder (OCD). It includes progressively exposing people to the situations or thoughts that they dread while keeping them from responding in the compulsive manner that they are accustomed to.

- The objective is to convince individuals that their anxieties are unreasonable and that they are capable of enduring discomfort without reverting to their customary practices or the behaviors they have learned to avoid.

CBT provides clients with actionable coping methods that may be used to effectively control their anxiety, and this is one of its primary goals. Techniques for relaxation, such as deep breathing and progressive muscle relaxation, as well as mindfulness practices and abilities for stress management, are included in these tactics.

Homework Assignments: - Cognitive behavioral therapy frequently includes homework assignments that enable clients to practice and apply the skills taught in treatment to real-world circumstances outside of the therapy session. This helps encourage new ways of thinking and doing, which in turn is helpful.

Keeping Track of Your Progress: - In CBT, keeping track of your progress is often done with the help of instruments such as anxiety or mood diaries. Individuals keep a log of their thoughts, feelings, and behaviors in order to recognize patterns, as well as gauge their level of progress over time.

Taking a Look at Underlying basic Beliefs: - Cognitive behavioral therapy dives at underlying basic beliefs that may contribute to anxious feelings. Self-criticism, perfectionism, or a general feeling of ineptitude are all examples of the kinds of deeply established attitudes that fall under this category.

- Individuals can experience substantial alterations in their perception of themselves and the world around them by questioning and revising the fundamental assumptions that underpin their worldview.

Relapse Prevention: Cognitive behavioral therapy places a strong emphasis on relapse prevention by instructing patients to notice early warning indicators of a recurrence of their anxiety and by providing methods to successfully manage and cope with challenging situations.

CBT is versatile and can be adapted to address diverse anxiety disorders, such as Generalized Anxiety Disorder (GAD),

Social Anxiety Disorder, Panic Disorder, and particular phobias. Because of its adaptability, CBT is an effective treatment for a wide range of anxiety disorders.

Long-Term Benefits: - Research has shown that the benefits of CBT extend beyond the therapy session, with many people getting long-term alleviation from anxiety symptoms as a result of receiving treatment with CBT.

Combined Methods: - Cognitive behavioral therapy (CBT) may, in certain instances, be used in conjunction with medication, particularly for severe anxiety disorders. Both of these strategies have the potential to work together to form a more comprehensive treatment strategy.

In general, cognitive behavioral therapy is an extremely useful and adaptable method for the management of anxiety. It provides individuals with the knowledge, resources, and skills necessary to recognize, confront, and ultimately conquer anxious thoughts and behaviors, which ultimately results in increased mental well-being and a higher quality of life.

Incorporating Mindfulness: Some Useful Pointers And Advice

People who are interested in harnessing the power of mindfulness in order to better manage their anxiety may find the following practical recommendations helpful:

1. Take Baby Steps: To ease into the practice of mindfulness, start with shorter sessions and work your way up to longer ones as your comfort level with the technique increases.

2. Be Consistent: If you want to receive the advantages of mindfulness, you need to be consistent in your practice. Having consistent practice, even if it's only for a short period of time, can make a major difference over time.

3. Paying attention to one's breath while practicing mindfulness is considered to

be one of the primary mindfulness meditations. Focusing your consciousness on the sensations of breathing can serve as a grounding device that brings you back to the here and now.

4. Body Scan: The fourth type of meditation is called the body scan, and it consists of carefully directing your attention to different parts of the body and observing feelings without passing judgment on them. It has the potential to make you more sensitive to the physical manifestations of anxiety. 5. Engage in Mindful Observation: One way to practice mindful observation is to fully immerse oneself in the routines of daily life. Whether you are enjoying a meal or going for a walk, it is important to pay attention to the various sensory elements that each moment has to offer.

6. Guided Meditation: Beginning meditators often benefit from having sessions of guided meditation taught by more seasoned teachers who can offer structure and instruction.

7. applications for Mindfulness: Investigate applications for mindfulness that provide guided sessions and exercises for mindfulness. These apps typically incorporate tracking capabilities so you can keep tabs on your development.

8. Practicing Mindfulness in Everyday Life: Take your mindfulness training beyond the confines of formal practice. Incorporate attentive awareness into tasks that are already part of your routine, such as eating, driving, or working.

9. Self-Compassion In order to cultivate self-compassion, you should show yourself love and understanding at all times, but especially when you are feeling anxious.

10. Participate in Mindfulness Classes or Seek help From a Mindfulness Instructor or Therapist To further your practice of mindfulness, you should participate in mindfulness classes or seek help from a mindfulness instructor or therapist.

Practices That Can Help Clear Your Mind And Reduce The Mental Clutter You Experience On A Day-To-Day Basis Include:

Emotional, psychological, and social well-being are all important aspects that contribute to an individual's overall mental health. It has an effect on our thoughts, feelings, actions, decisions, and how we connect with other people. The absence of mental illness is only one aspect of mental health; rather, it is the ability to function normally mentally that is essential to one's overall health and quality of life. If you suffer from a mental illness, engaging in self-care activities can help you preserve your mental health, which in turn can make your treatment and recovery more successful.

Regarding the Practice of Self-Care

Practicing self-care is devoting some of your time and energy to undertaking endeavors that will benefit not just your bodily but also your mental and emotional well-being. When it comes to your mental health, practicing self-care can help you better manage stress, lower your chance of getting sick, and give you a greater sense of vitality. It's amazing how much of a difference can be made by incorporating even a few simple self-care practices into your daily routine.

To help you get started with practicing self-care, here are some pointers:

Make regular time for some form of physical activity:

Walking for at least half an hour on a daily basis can assist improve both your mood and your physical health. Do not lose up on your goal of becoming more physically active if you are unable to exercise for a whole thirty minutes at a time.

Eat balanced meals on a regular basis and make sure you stay hydrated:

Maintaining your energy level and mental clarity throughout the day will be easier if you eat well and drink lots of water. Reduce the amount of caffeinated beverages, such as coffee and soft drinks, that you consume during the day.

Make getting enough sleep your number one priority:

Keep to your schedule, and give yourself plenty of time to sleep every night. Because exposure to blue light from electronic devices and displays might make it difficult to fall asleep, you should try to limit the amount of time you spend looking at your phone or computer screen before bed.

Consider engaging in a calming activity:

Explore several applications or programs that can help you relax or improve your health. Some examples of these programs include meditation, activities to relax your muscles, and breathing exercises. Make time in your schedule for these activities as well as other enjoyable and beneficial hobbies, such as writing.

Determine your goals and order your priorities:

Identify the tasks that require immediate attention and those that can wait. Learn to use the word "no" when it comes to new initiatives if you find that you are already taking on too much. At the end of the day, you should make an effort to reflect on what you have been successful in achieving rather than what you have not been able to achieve.

Gratitude should be practiced:

Make it a daily habit to bring to mind all of the blessings for which you are thankful. Put up your argument. You can either jot them down or play them back in your head before going to bed.

Focus your attention on the positive:

Recognize and combat the unhelpful and unproductive thoughts you have.

Continue to keep the connection.

Make contact with friends or family members who not only can provide assistance in a practical sense, but also emotional support.

Everyone has their own idea of what constitutes "self-care," and it is essential to figure out what you want as well as what you need. Finding out what works best for you could need some experimentation and exploration of other options. In addition, although self-care is not a therapy for mental illnesses, it can assist you in managing your mental health by assisting you in determining what causes or triggers your mild symptoms as well as what coping strategies are most effective for you.

Increasing One's Own Self-Esteem

Your level of self-esteem is the sum total of all of the ideas you have when you reflect on how confident you are in your own abilities. If you have healthy levels of self-esteem, you are likely to have greater levels of self-confidence than someone who does not. Low self-esteem is especially common among people who are prone to engaging in self-criticism. Low self-esteem is a common contributor to mental health conditions like depression and anxiety.

CBT is one of the most effective treatment approaches available for a wide variety of psychiatric problems. It is a concise type of treatment that targets the fundamental issues that you are now struggling with. CBT is different from other treatment methods since it focuses on the things that are causing you difficulty right now, as opposed to discussing relationships and your early developmental history.

Any one of the following cognitive behavioral therapy (CBT) procedures may be included in the treatment for low self-esteem:

• Assertiveness Training • Cognitive Restructuring • Behavioral Experiments and Activation • Problem-Solving Took an approach. This wasn't always in this spot; it was previously defined down below.

• Training in mindfulness. • Developing one's social skills. Everything that is marked in yellow does not have a definition below, yet it has been put here.

• Study of the existing schema • Playing roles in a simulated setting

Reorganization of Thoughts and Concepts

Your therapist will aim to detect negative thought patterns and then replace them with positive thought patterns as part of the cognitive restructuring process. Identifying the unfavorable things you believe about yourself and your capabilities is an important step in building your self-esteem. It is about discovering the flaws in your way of thinking and correcting them.

There will be numerous occasions in which you may have the feeling that you are a failure in life. This may be due to the fact that you are lacking in certain abilities or just because you are having a terrible day. You should not let these things get you down. Negative self-talk will only serve to make the situation much more difficult. You should not let this go to your head because even the best of people have bad days occasionally.

Activation of Behavioural Patterns

If you have a low sense of self-esteem, you will avoid going to locations or participating in activities that make you feel uncomfortable. Anything in which you have a sneaking suspicion that you might not do particularly well will naturally go lower on your list of priorities. The problem with this is that it will continue to reduce the number of possibilities you have to participate in enriching activities. Such inclinations almost always result in clinical depression.

Within the context of the behavioral activation process, your therapist will assist you in breaking this pattern of negative behavior. Your therapist will assist you re-engage with particular social circles in which you have become disengaged, reconnect with those circles, and enjoy some of the most enriching experiences that you have been deprived of because of this disconnection.

Unlocking your full potential with strategies for more efficient time management.

The ability to structure one's time in a methodical and organized manner is a crucial talent that helps direct individuals toward the achievement of their objectives and facilitate their progression.

On the other hand, a lot of people have trouble managing their time properly, which can result in stress and worry as well as a reduction in productivity. Changing your perspective, developing self-discipline and motivation, overcoming procrastination and other time-wasting behaviors, and learning the benefits of excellent time management are some of the topics that will be covered in this section.

Shift your mentality and adopt a proactive approach to managing your time.

A proactive approach to time management is required in order to effectively schedule strategic blocks of time. In order to accomplish this, you will need to define your objectives and top priorities, devise a timetable, and work on methods to deal with interruptions and diversions. Taking personal responsibility for your time and acknowledging the significance of efficiently managing that time are both essential components of a proactive strategy for time management. People can begin to take charge of their time and achieve their goals in a more effective manner by adopting a proactive mindset and mentality.

The importance of both self-discipline and motivation in achieving goals

The ability to effectively manage one's time requires core components such as self-discipline and motivation. Self-discipline refers to the ability to reign in one's desires and maintain concentration on significant responsibilities, especially when doing so is neither pleasurable nor simple. The desire to accomplish one's objectives and triumph over challenges is an essential component of motivation. Self-discipline and motivation can be helpful in maintaining one's concentration and level of production in spite of interruptions or other impediments.

Conquering procrastination and other time-wasting behaviors can be accomplished with these strategies.

Habits of procrastination and squandering time can be significant roadblocks on the path to efficient time management. Nevertheless, people can overcome these problems with the help of a few different tactics, including the following:

Tasks should be broken down into smaller, more achievable segments.

By subdividing a task into a number of smaller steps, one might make the process feel less daunting and find it easier to manage. People who struggle with procrastination and difficulty maintaining focus on their goals may benefit from doing this.

Create a timetable for yourself.

The development of a program can assist individuals in more successfully managing their time and avoiding the habit of procrastination. In addition to this, it can assist in ensuring that vital chores are finished on time.

Take away any distractions: People may find it easier to concentrate and get more work done if they get rid of distractions like social media and email notifications. This can help improve overall time management and reduce the amount of time spent putting things off.

Acknowledge and reward achievement

People can maintain their motivation and concentration on their goals with the support of rewarding progress made toward those goals. By giving you a feeling of success and satisfaction when you finish something, this can assist you in overcoming habits of procrastination and wasting time.

How efficient management of one's time can liberate latent inner potential

By assisting people in more effectively achieving their objectives, efficient management of time can help individuals realize their full potential. People who are able to properly manage their time are better able to concentrate on key work and steer clear of distractions, both of which can contribute to improvements in productivity and performance. People who effectively manage their time may also find that they have less stress and worry, which is beneficial to their general well-being and quality of life.

The Impact of Hormones Related to Stress

Anxiety is complicated and diverse, and one factor that contributes to it is the hormones that are released in response to stress, specifically cortisol and adrenaline. Chronic or excessive activation of the stress response can contribute to the development of anxiety disorders as well as the worsening of symptoms associated with existing anxiety disorders. Stress hormones are a natural aspect of the body's response to perceived threats or stressors. A closer look reveals the following about the connection between stress hormones and anxious feelings:

The activation of the "fight or flight" response includes the following: The "fight or flight" reaction is responsible for the release of stress hormones in the body. This response helps the body get ready to deal with any perceived dangers. For instance, adrenaline quickens the heart rate, makes it easier to concentrate, and releases latent energy. This response can be adaptive in circumstances of acute stress, so assisting individuals in effectively responding to problems that they face.

Enhanced Signs and Symptoms of Anxiety: Even though the stress response is supposed to improve both a person's physical and mental readiness, it can also cause symptoms that are more frequently associated with anxiety. The release of adrenaline can often cause individuals to experience feelings of agitation, anxiousness, and even panic under certain circumstances. These symptoms might be confusing since they resemble those of an anxiety disorder, and they can also contribute to increased worry.

Dysregulation can be caused by chronic stress, which occurs when the body's stress response system is overstimulated for an extended period of time. Particularly high amounts of the stress hormone cortisol have been connected to several anxiety disorders. since of this, prolonged exposure to stress can desensitize the body to the effects of cortisol, which can lead to increased anxiety since the body becomes less responsive to the natural regulatory mechanisms it possesses.

influence on Brain Structure and Function Both chronic stress and increased cortisol levels have the potential to have an influence on the structure and function of the brain. This can include alterations in the amygdala, an area of the brain involved in the processing of emotions, as well as changes in the prefrontal cortex, a region of the brain that plays a role in decision-making as well as the control of emotions. These modifications may be a factor in increased anxiety as well as a reduction in one's capacity to properly regulate that worry.

Anxiety itself can further worsen the stress reaction and cortisol release, which creates a feedback loop in the body. Individuals who suffer from anxiety disorders frequently experience worry and fear about their symptoms, which can lead to greater stress and a recurrence of the anxiety symptoms that they already experience.

Conditions Related to Anxiety: Chronic exposure to elevated levels of stress hormones has been linked to the development of anxiety disorders like generalized anxiety disorder (GAD) and post-traumatic stress disorder (PTSD), as well as the worsening of symptoms associated with these conditions. In patients with these conditions, the mechanism that controls the stress response becomes dysregulated, which results in persistent and extreme anxiety.

Implications for Treatment
Understanding the function that stress hormones play in anxiety is critical for developing effective treatment strategies. Individuals may find it easier to cope with anxiety by employing strategies such as cognitive behavioral therapy (CBT), mindfulness, and stress reduction that target both the psychological and physiological parts of the disease. In some instances, a patient may also be administered antidepressants or other types of medication that works to control the hormones that are released in response to stress.

In conclusion, the persistent activation of stress hormones, despite the fact that they are a normal and adaptive aspect of the body's response to stress, can contribute to the development of anxiety disorders as well as the worsening of existing ones. It is essential to get an understanding of the dynamic relationship between stress hormones and anxiety in order to develop effective treatments for anxiety that address both the physiological and psychological elements of the condition and, as a result, lead to improved mental health.

Share What You Have To Offer With The World.

The benefit of being a part of a community is having people around us on whom we can rely for support as we make our way through the many stages of our lives. On the other hand, giving back to our community and finding opportunities to share our talents, knowledge, and experience with others may be extremely gratifying endeavors in and of themselves. The fact that providing value to others in a selfless manner can lead to the development of a profound sense of personal fulfillment is an intriguing phenomenon. The reward for being helpful to another person and assisting them in achieving their Ikigai is to experience this nice sensation and positive energy as a result of your efforts. When it comes to adding value to the lives of others, keep these three things in mind:

Have some guts, people!

To be able to contribute to the success of another individual or organization, you will first need the bravery to come forward and recognize the value that you, yourself, bring to the table. If you want to reach out to another person and share your skills, expertise, or talents with them, you might need the confidence to make the initial contact or take the first step in doing so. In a personal setting, this could mean having the bravery to offer guidance to a friend on a subject in which you have experience. In a professional setting, this could mean having the courage to suggest a new concept that can benefit the company or to offer your aid to a colleague who appears to be overwhelmed. Putting yourself out there might possibly have an effect that lasts a lifetime, and all it takes is crazy courage and twenty seconds of your time.

Please Don't Keep It to Yourself!

It's easy to take for granted how much information you have stored in your brain. This is especially true in situations in which you are surrounded by other intelligent people who might know just as much as you do and, as a result, might not appear to have any need for your assistance. However, the fact of the matter is that what you know can be helpful to other people who want to do the same things that you have been able to do. Finding others who are interested in being mentored or in having their knowledge shared is one way to grow your community.

Maintain Your Focus on Improving Yourself.

When you can't recognize the value you possess, you can't help other people in any meaningful way. In order to teach others about your abilities, knowledge, and skills, you must first have complete faith in who you are and acknowledge the value of what you bring to the table. How you look at yourself is important because it might be the factor that either enables you to extend yourself to others or prevents you from doing so. You will be able to add more value to anything you do for other people if you put the effort into figuring out your own passions and talents, as well as your own passions and limitations.

Things That People Who Suffer From Social Anxiety Want To Have

Simply the fact that you suffer from social anxiety does not distinguish you in any way from other people. You, like them, want to have meaningful connections with other people, you want to be successful, and you want your life to be peaceful. You are also looking for other people to have some level of comprehension. This is an excellent list to show those who just don't seem to grasp your situation or who don't understand why you have to battle if you come into contact with those people. Those of you who struggle with anxiety disorders could recognize themselves in my descriptions of the following situations:

1. The Relationship

People who have social anxiety disorder may have a dread of being in social situations, facing other people, or engaging in social interaction; despite this, however, they still desire to have friends. When someone is alone himself for an extended period of time, they may experience feelings of depression and loneliness. We as humans are social beings, and in order for us to thrive, we require the company of others. You will be able to conquer your anxiety if you get the appropriate treatment and work on improving your social skills. You are not the only one to experience this; when we try to become friends with a new person, we all feel a little bit uneasy, but it does get easier over time.

2. Having an awareness of

A person who suffers from social anxiety disorder wants to be heard more than anything else in the world. They want to be understood, not just as a person, but also with regard to their symptoms and the challenges they experience on a daily basis. This is something they want more than anything else in the world. If you are attempting to understand and assist a friend or family member who suffers from an anxiety condition, it can be helpful to learn more about the disorder itself. If you have the condition and are surrounded by others who do not understand it, you may want to consider publishing an article that explains it or leaving a book that discusses it lying around the house.

3. Solitude A person who suffers from social anxiety often has a strong need to interact with other people, but they also have a requirement to spend time alone on a regular basis. Introversion and social anxiety can coexist at times, and when this happens, it's a good idea to take some time to yourself to recharge your batteries and gather your strength before attempting to engage with others again. While extroverts draw their energy from being among other people, introverts, on the other hand, require time alone to recharge their batteries and feel better about themselves. Even if you're in the thick of a social event, if you're an introvert, you shouldn't feel

bad about requiring some time to yourself. Don't apologize for it. Even though our culture places a higher value on extroverted personalities, there is absolutely nothing wrong with being an introvert. If everyone in the world had an outgoing personality, it would make the world a very unsettling place to live. Consider the implications!

4. a stable environment

In particular, emotional stability, which is one of the most important things for many people who struggle with social anxiety disorder to achieve. Some people want to be able to better manage their feelings, thoughts, and emotions, and they want to know exactly what sets off their anxiety symptoms so that they may avoid such things in the future. They are interested in learning how they can keep their feelings in check when they are put in such kinds of circumstances. Instead of trying to exert control over the worry, it is sometimes more beneficial to simply let it pass and become at one with your sensations.

The demand for stability stems from the same source as the need to avoid change, which was previously discussed in relation to persons who suffer from seasonal affective disorder (SAD). When things are stable, the future becomes more predictable. Even in terms of emotional steadiness, this is true. If you are able to anticipate how you will behave at the next social gathering that you go to, you will likely feel considerably more at ease about attending to that event. If you are able to forecast how others will behave at that gathering, you will likely feel much more at ease as well.

5. Quiet and rest

If you suffer from social anxiety, you should know that there are a number of strategies that might help you find calm. You may try something like yoga, mindfulness meditation, deep breathing, or some other practice that is intended to help you become more aware of your surroundings and more in sync with your body. One of the treatments that isavailable is called acceptance and commitment therapy, and it is one of the therapies that can assist you in making the most of these kinds of exercises while you are working on lessening the symptoms of your anxiety.

When looking to achieve peace, religion is another factor that must be ignored. Numerous studies have been done to demonstrate that religious people, in general, report higher levels of happiness and contentment, which contributes significantly to the promotion of peace.

6. A sense of assurance

Confidence may be the most important thing to certain people who struggle with anxiety disorders. Your level of self-assurance will only increase if you are willing to confront your anxieties and actively work toward overcoming them. Confront the things in your life that cause you anxiety, and work methodically on boosting your self-confidence. In due time, the factors that first brought on your symptoms will have less of an impact, and you will develop the self-assurance necessary to deal with the situation.

Practice and the realization that one is capable of achieving one's goals are also key components in the development of confidence. Both of these activities require going out into the world and talking to different kinds of people. If you never venture outside of your home, you won't be able to perfect anything or make any progress.

7. Satisfaction of needs

Some people who suffer from social anxiety disorder have the perception that they will never be able to accomplish the things they set out to do due of their condition. This prevents them from experiencing the same level of contentment with their existence. Everyone needs a purpose in life, and everyone needs objectives; being able to overcome one's fears and accomplish one's goals can bring to a genuine feeling of contentment and success.

8. Development

A significant number of individuals who suffer from social anxiety disorder are interested in advancing their own personal development. They will look at other people's experiences about how they overcame their concerns and read any self-help books that are available to them in order to understand how to develop themselves and become better individuals. This is a really healthy ambition to have, as continuing your education and making an effort to develop yourself will undoubtedly make the path to recovery simpler for you.

Physical Experiences While Surfing

Both depression and anxiety are accompanied by a wide range of mental and physical symptoms. The experiences are frequently terrifying and exceptionally powerful. If you've ever suffered from panic attacks, there's a good chance that you're familiar with a number of the symptoms associated with them.

It is simple for you to misinterpret the feelings you have in your body as serious or life-threatening indications that anything is wrong with your health. If you do not recognize the mental and physical feelings you are experiencing as being caused by anxiety, you are likely to make the false assumption that you are going insane, having an attack, being unable to breathe, passing out, or maybe dying.

It is not inconceivable that somebody would want to put an end to their symptoms and work on finding a way to control them. Unfortunately, these efforts to combat the physical symptoms associated with hysteria usually invariably have the result of making the situation even more ludicrous. One ends up becoming too concerned about their nervous sensations, and in an effort to control or get rid of them, they wind up making the situation even more difficult for themselves and contributing further to the problem. Behaviors that are intended to prevent, minimize, or lessen the intensity of physical sensations are examples of what are known as "safety behaviors."

You should consult your psychiatrist if you believe that you have a genuine health problem that requires further evaluation. It is always essential for you to retain a clean bill of health before entering yourself into the exposure exercises; this may assist you eliminate the bothersome bodily symptoms that come along with hysteria.

Walking a great distance away from A burden to bear Worry

When someone has a mental illness, the likelihood that they may experience anxiety is increased significantly. The majority of the time, every person will experience anxiety from time to time. The only way to stop worrying about everything at once is to stop caring about anything. Nevertheless, there is a significant gap between anxiety that is not healthy and concern that is beneficial to one's well-being. The first step involves pointless worries and feelings of terror. Worrying so much that it consumes the majority of our time and energy is counterproductive and can bring on feelings of anxiousness.

If you become aware that the problems that are most prominent and persistent for you do, in fact, repeatedly return, although in somewhat different ways, this indicates that you have some distinct worry themes. Because of this, it is likely that you worry an excessive amount about these aspects of your life, even when there is nothing in particular to be concerned about. Relationships, money, health, and the thoughts of others are among the most prominent sources of anxiety for people. If you have been worrying for a significant amount of time, there is a good chance that you are just unaware of the fact that you may educate your mind to be free from the ideas and feelings of worry through a process known as cognitive retraining. It's possible that worrying too much is a bad habit, but if you keep at it with determination and fortitude, you can break the cycle. To overcome it will need a lot of sacrifices and hard work, but the reward will be worth it in the end. When someone breaks their habit of worrying, they often report feeling exposed and out of place as a result. However, in a short period of time, you will become accustomed to the pleasant release that comes with no longer being a persistent worrier. Don't give yourself too much time to be anxious about the situation. In order to prevent anxious thoughts from occupying your mind, you should become involved in a variety of events and activities.

Pick out things to do that need your full attention, such as doing the books, taking notes on others, or putting together a puzzle. Exercising regularly can be extremely beneficial for you in a variety of ways and can even help you "sweat out" your concerns.

www.ingramcontent.com/pod-product-compliance
Lightning Source LLC
Chambersburg PA
CBHW052134110526
44591CB00012B/1717